THE HERITAGE COLLECTION

TAYTU BETUL

THE LIGHT OF ETHIOPIA

Letitia deGraft Okyere

Illustrated by Zunaira Shabbir

Lion's Historian PRESS
Amplifying Authentic Voices

Taytu Betul: The Light of Ethiopia

Copyright © 2021 by Letitia deGraft Okyere

Illustrator: Zunaira Shabbir

Interior layout designer: Nasim Malik Sarkar

Library of Congress Control Number: 2021925086

All rights reserved.

No part of this publication may be reproduced, stored in a retrieval system, a database and/or published in any form or by any means, electronic, mechanical, photocopying, recording or otherwise, without the prior written permission of the publisher.

ISBN 978-1-7374048-6-6 hardback
ISBN 978-1-7374048-7-3 ebook

Published by Lion's Historian Press
https://www.lionshistorian.net/

For

Anima and Yaw Asiama

CONTENTS

A Proud Ethiopian 1

From Childhood to Adult 3

Queen Taytu 5

Trouble Brews with Italy 7

Founding of Addis Ababa 9

Taytu's Courage 11

The Treaty of Wuchale 13

Empress Taytu 15

Advisor to the Emperor Menilek II 17

Treaty Deception Uncovered 19

War with Italy 21

Post War Years 23

A Reflection of Empress Taytu's Life 25

Glossary 27

Quiz 28

References 29

Other Books in the Heritage Collection 30

Read about Yaa Asantewaa 31

Chapter 1

A Proud Ethiopian

Taytu Betul, whose name means *sunshine*, was a descendant of the powerful Emperor Susenyos of Ethiopia. Historians believe Taytu was born in the early 1850s. Her mother's name was Yewubdar. Taytu's father, Betul Hayle Maryam, was a military officer. Taytu had two older brothers, Wele and Alulua, and a younger sister called Desta.

Destiny had a hand on Taytu because her parents ensured she was well educated, at a time when only boys enjoyed that privilege. Taytu learned how to read and write Amharic and was fluent in the Ethiopian classical language called *Geez*. Taytu took classes in many subjects, like law, business, and international diplomacy.

When Taytu took time from her studies, she played chess, winning against male opponents, including her brothers. Taytu enjoyed music, learning how to play the musical instrument called the *begenna* and composing poetry.

From Childhood to Adult

Taytu's mother, Yewubdar, began to prepare her early for marriage. This meant Taytu's time running freely in the fields with her friends ended. Instead, her mother gave her cooking lessons and other training on how to keep a home.

Soon, Taytu was married to her first husband, an officer to Emperor Tewodros of Ethiopia. This marriage ended badly when the Emperor Tewodros put Taytu's husband in chains, while he forced Taytu to walk behind the army on foot.

Taytu's subsequent marriages also brought her hardship; however, she never gave up on life. During these difficult years, often, she had to sleep unprotected in the bitter cold, carry heavy loads bare foot and nurse wounds of warriors.

Queen Taytu

On April 29, 1883, when Taytu was about thirty years old, she married King Menilek of Shewa, a southern kingdom within Ethiopia. The two were married in Ankober, the capital of Shewa. Unlike Menilek's previous marriages, this was a full communion ceremony meaning they could never be divorced.

Decades earlier, when Menilek was a Prince of Shewa, he had met Taytu's brothers when all three were prisoners of war. Menilek had shown an interest in marrying Taytu because he admired Taytu's older brothers. However, the Betul family did not think the marriage would create a worthy alliance for the family and refused Menilek's offer.

In 1883 though, this marriage created an important northern and southern alliance, increasing Menilek's political power and making Taytu influential in Menilek's government. When the Ethiopian Emperor Yohannes summoned King Menilek for a conference, he was accompanied by Queen Taytu because Menilek appreciated Taytu's sharp intellect.

Trouble Brews with Italy

At the time of Taytu's marriage in 1883, King Menilek was deepening his relationship with Italy through a diplomat called Count Pietro Antonelli. The relationship with Antonelli resulted in a Treaty between Shewa and Italy, allowing mutual diplomatic exchanges, freedom of movement and trade. Taytu did not stop the Treaty of 21 May 1883, but she ensured that the Amharic translation was accurate, removing any clauses allowing Italy to exploit Shewa.

In early 1885, Italian troops took control of the port of Massawa, affecting Ethiopian interests. An angry Taytu agreed with Ethiopia's Emperor Yohanne's request for Menilek to remove Antonelli from Shewa.

Antonelli successfully negotiated a cancellation of the order while he tried to build a relationship with Queen Taytu. However, Taytu's distrust of the Europeans began to grow.

8

Founding of Addis Ababa

After the marriage, Queen Taytu asked to build a church dedicated to St. Mary at Entotto, in the highlands of Shewa. Menilek agreed to Taytu's request. Taytu also began to establish Entotto as her capital, adopting "red" as the color of her royal household and making sure it was visible around Entotto. Taytu also became known for her charitable works to the poor and needy.

After the Entotto feast in October 1887 to dedicate the Maryam Church, the court went down the highlands to the hot springs for relaxation. Taytu enjoyed the area, which was not as cold as Entotto, and had better water supply.

Taytu encouraged her husband to call the place Addis Ababa, meaning *the new flower*. The mimosa trees were in full bloom displaying its beautiful flowers. Addis Ababa became Menilek's new capital, and Entotto, the home of the Church and place for religious celebrations.

Addis Ababa was completed within two years. Today, Addis Ababa is Ethiopia's largest city with a population of close to three million.

Taytu's Courage

Taytu soon demonstrated her courage when King Menilek went to war against Harar in the east, in 1887. Menilek left Taytu in charge of Shewa, who was in Addis Ababa, where Menilek's army had gathered.

Soldiers who were supposed to meet with King Menilek deserted the battle and began to return to Addis Ababa. Though Taytu was angry about the desertion, she saw an opportunity to stock up military supplies. Thus, she wisely sent them a message of welcome if they were returning to guard her.

In the meantime, she asked governors in neighboring provinces to take all guns and military equipment from the deserters as supplies were running low. When the deserters arrived at Addis Ababa, Queen Taytu gave them passes to the governors she had made agreements with. They easily walked into the trap set by the queen.

Ethiopians were impressed by how Taytu handled the deserters. Menilek successfully took Harar, assisted by the supplies skillfully taken from the deserters.

The Treaty of Wuchale

When Ethiopian Emperor Yohannes died from war injuries in March 1889, King Menilek, with Taytu's support, declared himself the new Emperor of Ethiopia. On Taytu's advice, Menilek quickly obtained oaths of loyalty from as many Ethiopian governors as possible.

During this time, Menilek signed the Treaty of Wuchale with Italian emissary Antonelli on May 2, 1889. It allowed the Italians to establish a new colony called Eritrea and helped Menilek to strengthen his hold over Ethiopia.

However, Article 17 of the Treaty had two versions. The Amharic text protected the sovereign rights of Ethiopia, with only diplomatic relations with Italy. The Italian version made Ethiopia a subject of Italy. The difference would lead to war between Ethiopia and Italy.

Empress Taytu

Unfortunately, in 1889, there was a bad famine and life became difficult for Ethiopians. Queen Taytu and King Menilek made a holy pilgrimage to the Holy Stone Churches in Lalibela to ask God for mercy. Lalibela is an important place in Ethiopia; considered one of the wonders of the world. It was built in the 13th century to be a representation of Jerusalem.

Empress Taytu had a shelter constructed to provide water and food to the homeless and hungry Ethiopians. She encouraged those who were better off to help with feeding programs. Empress Taytu also established other camps, feeding and tending to the poor.

On November 5, 1889, Taytu was crowned Empress, two days after Menilek was crowned Emperor of Ethiopia, styled as Menilek II. Empress Taytu was officially addressed as the *Light of Ethiopia* and her personal seal bore these words.

Advisor to the Emperor Menilek II

The famine finally ceased after several years and the Empress began to build alliances across the empire, becoming a valued advisor to the emperor. Empress Taytu had business interests which she managed efficiently, in addition to palace operations.

Emperor Menilek II trusted Taytu's decisions and supported her administrative, military, political and international relations activities. Taytu and Menilek II worked well together. When Menilek was unable to make difficult decisions or those that had unfavorable consequences, he relied on his Empress to make the needed change.

Empress Taytu demonstrated loyalty to the country. She led efforts to preserve Ethiopian's cultural heritage. She assisted Emperor Menilek II with bridge, library, and railway projects. The greatest achievement was the installation of piped water in Addis Ababa. Empress Taytu became the most powerful woman in the country.

Chapter 10

Treaty Deception Uncovered

The deception with the Treaty of Wuchale was discovered by Empress Taytu. This was during a time when Italy refused to stay within the boundaries agreed. This time, negotiations with Count Antonelli failed to resolve the issue peacefully. Ethiopia would not give up its sovereignty to Italy.

The Italians also angered the Empress with plans to raise its flag in Ethiopian territory. She told Emperor Menilek II, "I am a woman and do not love war, but sooner than accept this I prefer war." When Count Antonelli informed the Empress that the breaking of Article 17 could cause Italy to lose its dignity. She replied, "we too must maintain our dignity. You want other countries to see Ethiopia as your protégé, but that will never be."

With Empress Taytu's support, Emperor Menilek ended the Treaty of Wuchale and refused to recognize Italian expansions in Ethiopia. Empress Taytu did not trust European intentions towards her country and she put a stop to diplomatic relationships with Italy.

Chapter 11

War with Italy

The Italians were not concerned about war with Ethiopia. While the Italian General returned to Italy on vacation, Empress Taytu prepared the Ethiopian army for war. On October 11, 1895, Empress Taytu and Emperor Menilek II with their armies, left Addis Ababa.

The Ethiopians were victorious at Amba Alage in December 1895. Next, the Ethiopians moved to the Italian fort at Meqelle. Empress Taytu recognized that a frontal attack would lead to a massacre of Ethiopian forces and she recommended a siege by controlling its water supply. Taytu got some 900 men from her contingent to implement her plan. In close to two weeks, the Italians surrendered and Ethiopians raised their flag over the Italian fort.

A month later, the Ethiopian victory was completed at the battle of Adwa, on March 1, 1896. Taytu displayed courage. She spoke to weary soldiers to remain strong and keep fighting. While bullets were firing all around, she lay prostrate on the ground praying for mercy. Taytu also commanded her cannoneers who fired furiously, successfully breaking the enemy's defenses.

Chapter 12

Post War Years

After preserving Ethiopia's sovereignty, Empress Taytu helped Emperor Menilek II to implement additional modernization projects. They improved communication and transportation across provinces and constructed buildings, churches, schools, hospitals, and industries.

Taytu also helped the Ethiopian religious community in Jerusalem, providing housing and financial support. Within Ethiopia, she helped to resolve religious differences in the Orthodox church. She inaugurated the Ethiopian Red Cross.

When Menilek II got sick in 1906, she made decisions on his behalf until 1910, when a regent was appointed until Menilek's death in 1913. Empress Taytu took a backseat from politics, retiring to her palace at Entotto. She died around age 70 years, on February 11, 1918. She was buried next to her husband at a monastery in Addis Ababa.

A Reflection of Empress Taytu's Life

Empress Taytu desired that Ethiopian interests should be protected above all. When she was Queen of Shewa, she supported the King and had the foresight to develop Addis Ababa's potential.

As Empress, she did not stay behind during the war with Italy. Taytu commanded her own army with 9,000 rifles, 600 horses, and four guns. Also, she traveled with a contingent of thousands of women who carried supplies for the war effort. Taytu organized food supplies from different provinces to feed the army. She encouraged men against retreat, motivated and mobilized thousands of women to fight and care for the wounded. Taytu managed the war's nerve center, receiving and analyzing information on Italian battle plans.

Empress Taytu's war strategy was effective in this historic battle where a native African army stopped a foreign country's expansion intentions. Taytu's determination to protect the dignity of her people was emulated by the great Queen Mother of Ejisu in Asante (present-day Ghana). This queen mother chose war with the British in 1900s, rather than allow Asante to be absorbed into the British empire.

Glossary

Amharic   Amharic is an Ethiopian language.

Begenna   The begenna is an Ethiopian instrument with ten strings like a lyre, common in ancient Greece.

Shewa   Shewa is a region in Ethiopia. The capital city Addis Ababa is in the center of Shewa.

Entotto   Entotto is the historical location where Taytu established a home. Now, it has many monasteries.

Mimosa tree   Mimosa trees covered the plains of what is now Addis Ababa. Its flowers inspired the name of the city.

Massawa   Massawa is a port city on the Red Sea in Eritrea. At a time, Ethiopia depended on the port.

Wuchale   The Treaty of Wuchale was signed between Ethiopia and Italy.

Lalibela   Lalibela is an important historic region in Ethiopia, the site of an ancient religious city.

Amba Alage   Amba Alage (or Imba Alaje) is a highland in Ethiopia where the Ethiopian army had victory over Italy in 1895.

Meqelle   Meqelle (or Mekelle) was the location for an Italian fort, seized by the Ethiopian army on instructions by Empress Taytu.

Quiz

1. How many siblings did Taytu Betul have?
   (a) 1
   (b) 2
   (c) 3
   (d) 4

2. What was the name of the Italian emissary who tried to build a relationship with Menilek?
   (a) Count Salimneni
   (b) Count Pedro Antonelli
   (c) Dr. Nerazzini
   (d) Count Traversi

3. What was the name of the treaty that led to war between Ethiopia and Italy?
   (a) Treaty of Shewa
   (b) Treaty of Entotto
   (c) Treaty of Meqelle
   (d) Treaty of Wuchale

4. Where did Empress Taytu's war strategy lead to a siege of an Italian fort?
   (a) Meqelle
   (b) Adwa
   (c) Amba Alage
   (d) Dessa

Quiz Answers: C,B,D,A

References

Prouty, Chris. *Empress Taytu and Menilek II: Ethiopia 1883-1910*. Trenton, Red Sea Press, 1986.

Tafla, Bairu. "Menilek II." *Encyclopedia Africana Dictionary of African Biography, Volume 1, Ethiopia – Ghana*, edited by L.H. Ofosu-Appiah, Reference Publications Inc., 1977, p. 108-110.

Rosenfeld, Chris Prouty. "Taytu Betul." *Encyclopedia Africana Dictionary of African Biography, Volume 1, Ethiopia – Ghana*, edited by L.H. Ofosu-Appiah, Reference Publications Inc., 1977, p. 136.

Other Books in the Heritage Collection

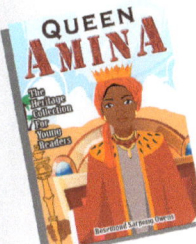

The story of Queen Amina is an important one for girls everywhere. Explore how Queen Amina gained a reputation as a fearless warrior, breaking barriers at a time when men dominated most aspects of life. Queen Amina's life will inspire and encourage you to be fearless.

Who was Queen Nandi? She is referred to as one of the greatest mothers that ever lived. As a queen mother, she saw her son Shaka become one of the greatest kings of the Zulu people and builder of the Zulu empire. Read her story and learn how she made her mark in history.

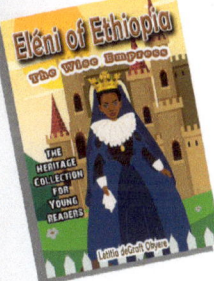

Eléni was a princess from Hadiya who became the wife of Emperor Zara Yaqob in 1445. Eléni guided the reign of five emperors and fearlessly challenged the leading role men played in society as an empress, queen mother and regent. Eléni's story will inspire girls and women everywhere to rise above difficult circumstances and fulfill their destiny.

R.J. Ghartey saw no limits to what he could achieve. As a young man, he rejected traditional paths of fishing and farming and learned a different trade. Through this, he became an influential business entrepreneur. In addition, Ghartey played an important role in local politics and found ways to improve the lives of those in his community. In telling Ghartey's story, the author hopes to encourage children with different dreams to pursue their destinies past challenges that they may face.

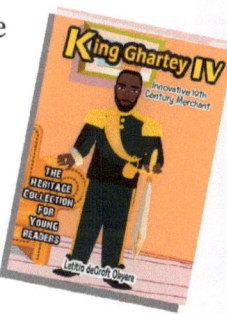

Read about Yaa Asantewaa

The Ethiopian victory in 1896 was important for Nationalists across Africa. Readers who enjoyed this story may be interested in *Yaa Asantewaa: The Fearless Queen*, also published by Lion's Historian Press in The Heritage Collection. It tells the story of Yaa Asantewaa, influenced by Taytu's courage to stand up for her people against British colonialism.

In the story of Queen Mother Yaa Asantewaa, the spirit of Empress Taytu comes alive. Yaa Asantewa, just like Taytu, agitated men to go to war rather than fall prey to colonial masters. Empress Taytu told men in her company that Ethiopia was going to fight the Italians. When her brother did not stand up in support of her statement, she said, "Here, you take my skirt and I will wear your trousers." Some ten years later, Yaa Asantewaa said to fellow Asante chiefs, "We will fight the white men. We will fight till the last of us falls on the battlefield. If you chiefs will not fight, you should exchange your loincloths for my undergarment."

Both leaders were commanders devising war strategy. They recruited women and motivated men to fight. Empress Taytu and Queen Mother Yaa Asantewaa were fierce in protecting national interests and demonstrating courage and dignity. Yaa Asantewaa followed Taytu in laying foundational tenets for the independence of Africa from colonial masters.

www.ingramcontent.com/pod-product-compliance
Lightning Source LLC
Chambersburg PA
CBHW041705160426
43209CB00017B/1748